Creative
PIANO SOLO

JAZZ POP SONGS

Unique, Distinctive Piano Arrangements of 20 Hit Songs

T0087270

ISBN 978-1-4950-7410-3

HAL•LEONARD®

7777 W. BLUEMOUND RD. P.O. BOX 13819 MILWAUKEE, WI 53213

Visit Hal Leonard Online at
www.halleonard.com

CONTENTS

DON'T KNOW WHY

Words and Music by
JESSE HARRIS

AFTER THE LOVE HAS GONE

Words and Music by DAVID FOSTER,
JAY GRAYDON and BILL CHAMPLIN

Slow and rhythmic, in 2

FEELING GOOD

from THE ROAR OF THE GREASEPAINT - THE SMELL OF THE CROWD

Words and Music by LESLIE BRICUSSE
and ANTHONY NEWLEY

HUMAN NATURE

Words and Music by JOHN BETTIS
and STEVE PORCARO

I JUST CALLED TO SAY I LOVE YOU

Words and Music by
STEVIE WONDER

Slowly, in 2

I PUT A SPELL ON YOU

Words and Music by
JAY HAWKINS

JUST THE TWO OF US

Words and Music by RALPH MacDONALD,
WILLIAM SALTER and BILL WITHERS

JUST THE WAY YOU ARE

Words and Music by
BILLY JOEL

KILLING ME SOFTLY WITH HIS SONG

Words by NORMAN GIMBEL
Music by CHARLES FOX

Gently flowing

THE LOOK OF LOVE
from CASINO ROYALE

Words and Music by HAL DAVID
and BURT BACHARACH

MACK THE KNIFE
FROM THE THREEPENNY OPERA

English Words by MARC BLITZSTEIN
Original German Words by BERT BRECHT
Music by KURT WEILL

Much broader, slower

poco accel.

STILL CRAZY AFTER ALL THESE YEARS

Words and Music by
PAUL SIMON

Moderate Latin

54

MICHELLE

Words and Music by JOHN LENNON
and PAUL McCARTNEY

SHOW ME THE WAY

Words and Music by
PETER FRAMPTON

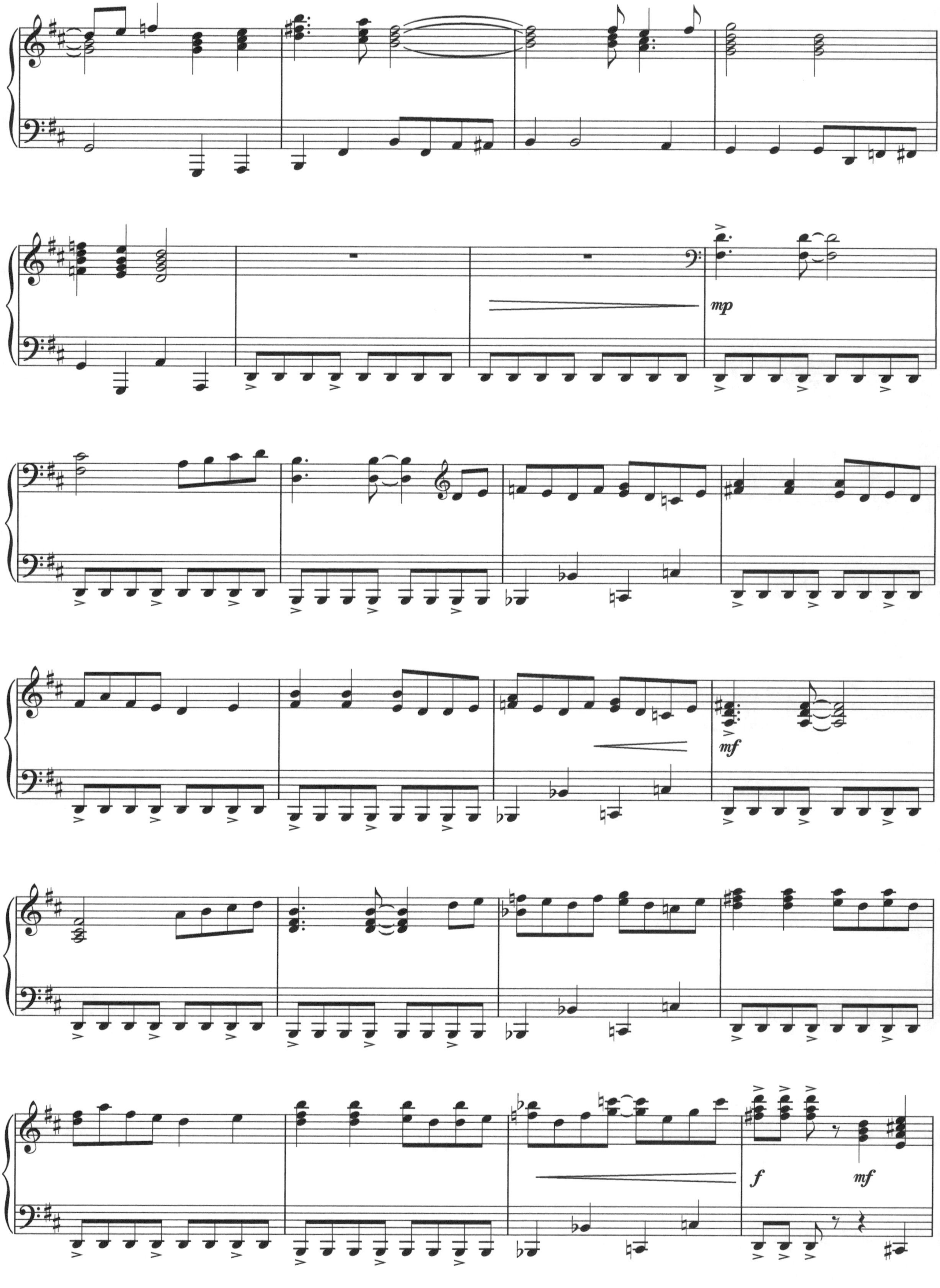
mp
mf
f
mf

SMOOTH OPERATOR

Words and Music by HELEN ADU
and RAY ST. JOHN

Power Ballad

To Coda ⊕

D.S. al Coda

CODA

SUNNY

Words and Music by
BOBBY HEBB

WHAT A WONDERFUL WORLD

Words and Music by GEORGE DAVID WEISS
and BOB THIELE

TAKE FIVE

By PAUL DESMOND

THIS GUY'S IN LOVE WITH YOU

Lyric by HAL DAVID
Music by BURT BACHARACH

WHAT YOU WON'T DO FOR LOVE

Words and Music by BOBBY CALDWELL
and ALFONS KETTNER

Creative PIANO SOLO

Looking to add some variety to your playing? Enjoy these beautifully distinctive arrangements for piano solo! These popular tunes get new and unique treatments for a fun and fresh presentation. Explore new styles and enjoy these favorites with a bit of a twist! Each collection includes 20 songs for the intermediate to advanced player.

BOHEMIAN RHAPSODY & OTHER EPIC SONGS

Band on the Run • A Day in the Life • Free Bird • November Rain • Piano Man • Roundabout • Stairway to Heaven • Take the Long Way Home • and more.

00196019 Piano Solo...**$14.99**

CHRISTMAS CAROLS

Away in a Manger • Deck the Hall • The First Noel • God Rest Ye Merry, Gentlemen • Hark! the Herald Angels Sing • It Came upon the Midnight Clear • Jingle Bells • Joy to the World • O Holy Night • Silent Night • Up on the Housetop • We Three Kings of Orient Are • What Child Is This? • and more.

00147214 Piano Solo...**$14.99**

CHRISTMAS COLLECTION

Blue Christmas • The Christmas Song (Chestnuts Roasting on an Open Fire) • Frosty the Snow Man • Here Comes Santa Claus (Right down Santa Claus Lane) • Let It Snow! Let It Snow! Let It Snow! • Silver Bells • Sleigh Ride • White Christmas • Winter Wonderland • and more.

00172042 Piano Solo...**$14.99**

CLASSIC ROCK

Another One Bites the Dust • Aqualung • Beast of Burden • Born to Be Wild • Carry on Wayward Son • Layla • Owner of a Lonely Heart • Roxanne • Smoke on the Water • Sweet Emotion • Takin' It to the Streets • 25 or 6 to 4 • Welcome to the Jungle • and more!

00138517 Piano Solo...**$14.99**

Prices, contents, and availability subject to change without notice.

DISNEY FAVORITES

Beauty and the Beast • Can You Feel the Love Tonight • Chim Chim Cher-ee • For the First Time in Forever • How Far I'll Go • Let It Go • Mickey Mouse March • Remember Me (Ernesto de la Cruz) • You'll Be in My Heart • You've Got a Friend in Me • and more.

00283318 Piano Solo...**$14.99**

JAZZ POP SONGS

Don't Know Why • I Just Called to Say I Love You • I Put a Spell on You • Just the Way You Are • Killing Me Softly with His Song • Mack the Knife • Michelle • Smooth Operator • Sunny • Take Five • What a Wonderful World • and more.

00195426 Piano Solo...**$14.99**

JAZZ STANDARDS

All the Things You Are • Beyond the Sea • Georgia on My Mind • In the Wee Small Hours of the Morning • The Lady Is a Tramp • Like Someone in Love • A Nightingale Sang in Berkeley Square • Someone to Watch Over Me • That's All • What'll I Do? • and more.

00283317 Piano Solo...**$14.99**

POP BALLADS

Against All Odds (Take a Look at Me Now) • Bridge over Troubled Water • Fields of Gold • Hello • I Want to Know What Love Is • Imagine • In Your Eyes • Let It Be • She's Got a Way • Total Eclipse of the Heart • You Are So Beautiful • Your Song • and more.

00195425 Piano Solo...**$14.99**

POP HITS

Billie Jean • Fields of Gold • Get Lucky • Happy • Ho Hey • I'm Yours • Just the Way You Are • Let It Go • Poker Face • Radioactive • Roar • Rolling in the Deep • Royals • Smells like Teen Spirit • Viva la Vida • Wonderwall • and more.

00138156 Piano Solo...**$14.99**

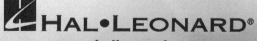

www.halleonard.com